US Special Operations Command in Action

MH-53J Pave Low from 21st SOS seen in Kurdistan during Operation *Provide Comfort.*

US Special Operations Command in Action

Patrick Allen

Airlife

A pair of MC-130 Combat Talons ripple-away flares over the sea.

First published in the UK in 2002
By Airlife Publishing Ltd

British Library Cataloguing-in-Publication Data
A catalogue record for this book
is available from the British Library

ISBN 1 84037 337 7

Typeset by Celtic, Wrexham
Printed in Hong Kong

For a complete list of all Airlife titles please contact:

Airlife Publishing Ltd
101 Longden Road, Shrewsbury, SY3 9EB, England
E-mail: sales@airlifebooks.com
Website: www.airlifebooks.com

ACKNOWLEDGMENTS

I would like to thank the following for their kind assistance in preparing this book: Major Thomas Collins at Headquarters US Army; Ms Carol Darby and S.Sgt Amanda Glenn at Headquarters ASOC; Elsie Jackson and all at Fort Benning and Camp Merrill; USAFSOC Headquarters and M.Sgt Chuck Roberts at RAF Mildenhall; Gy. Sgt Joseph P. Jascur at Headquarters USMC and Lt Michael Armistead, PAO and USMC photographers at 22D Marine Expeditionary Unit; Lt-Cdr Dawne Cutler at Headquarters US Navy and Navy Photo Division, Washington.

An MC-130H Combat Talon II refuels from a KC-135R tanker with the aid of NVGs.

CONTENTS

ACRONYMS

ALARP	–	Air Land Arming and Refuel Point
ASOC	–	Army Special Operations Command
BUD	–	Basic Underwater Demolition
CAS	–	Close Air Support
CCAD	–	Computer Controlled Air Drop
CCDS	–	Computer Controlled Drop System
CCT	–	Combat Control Team
CSAR	–	Combat Search and Rescue
CWT	–	Combat Weather Team
DAP	–	Direct Action Penetrator
ESS	–	External Stores System
EUCOM	–	European Command
FARP	–	Forward Arming and Refuel Point
FLIR	–	Forward Looking Infra–Red
FORB	–	Forward Operations and Refuelling Base
GMRS	–	Ground Marker Release System
HALO/HAHO	–	High Altitude Low Opening/High Altitude High Opening
HLS	–	Helicopter Landing Site
IDAS/MATT	–	Interactive Defence Avionics System/ Multi–Mission Advance Tactical Terminal
IQTC	–	Initial Qualifications Training Course
JFKSWCS	–	John F Kennedy Special Warfare Centre and School
JSOC	–	Joint Special Operations Command
LDA	–	Lateral Drift Apparatus
LDT	–	Lateral Drift Trainer
LRSLC	–	Long Range Surveillance Leaders Course
LRSP	–	Long Range Surveillance Patrol
LZ/DZ	–	Landing Zones/Drop Zones
MEU	–	Marine Expeditionary Unit
MFD	–	Multi-Function Display
MOUT	–	Military Operations in Urban Terrain

NEO	–	Non–Combatant Evacuation
NVG	–	Night Vision Goggles
PJ	–	Para–Jumper
RAP	–	Ranger Assessment Phase
RAWS	–	Ranger Anti–Tank Weapon System
RSOV	–	Ranger Special Operations Vehicle
RTU	–	Return to Unit
SAW	–	Squad Automatic Weapon
SCA	–	Self Contained Approach
SDV	–	SEAL Delivery Vehicle
SEAL	–	Sea Air and Land
SLT	–	Swing Landing Trainers
SOAR	–	Special Operations Aviation Regiment
SOC	–	Special Operations Capable
SOCEUR	–	Special Operations Command Europe
SOF	–	Special Operations Forces
SOG	–	Special Operations Group
SOP	–	Standard Operating Procedure
SOS	–	Special Operations Squadron
SOW	–	Special Operations Wing
STS	–	Special Tactics Squadron
SPIES/FRIES	–	Special Patrol Insertion/Extraction System and Fast Rope Insertion/Extraction System
TF/TA	–	Terrain Following/Terrain Avoidance
TRAP	–	Tactical Recovery of Aircraft and Personnel
TSOC	–	Theatre Special Operations Command
UAV	–	Unmanned Aerial Vehicle
UNOSOM	–	United Nations Operation Somalia
USAFSOC	–	United States Air Force Special Operations Command
USSOCM	–	United States Special Operations Command

INTRODUCTION

The US remains the world's dominant military power and continues to provide a global presence with US military operations and exercises taking place in over sixty countries around the world at any one time. Since the end of the Cold War, US forces have fought in Grenada, Panama, the Gulf War and Africa, and supported numerous peace-keeping and humanitarian operations worldwide including those in the Balkans as well as humanitarian missions in Kurdistan, Rwanda and Somalia.

With the end of the Cold War and a redefining of operational doctrine to meet changing military challenges, the US undertook a massive reduction in military force size in the late 1990s. New military doctrine now encompasses hard-hitting, flexible and easily deployable military forces

USMC special operations capable CH-46 and C-130 Hercules at a desert landing strip.

capable of undertaking a wide range of global missions including regional conflict, humanitarian and peace-keeping and disaster relief missions. The new force, although smaller, is better equipped, better trained and uses the latest military technology.

As the emphasis moves towards more rapidly deployable force structures, the role of US special operations has increased. Special operations are now at the forefront of US military operations and their personnel are the first to be deployed.

US Special Operations Command

The failure of Operation *Eagle's Claw*/Operation *Rice Bowl* to recover fifty-three US hostages held in Tehran during April 1980, and the subsequent disaster at 'Desert One' (the covert Forward Operating and Refuel Base (FORB)

established in the desert 265 miles east of Tehran), resulting in the death of eight people and the cancellation of the mission, led to a series of high level inquiries and commissions. These concluded that one of the problems was that the mission involved units from all four services (Army, Air Force, Navy, Marine Corps) that had never trained or worked together. The units operated unfamiliar equipment in aircraft that were not designed or equipped for special operations missions. Another problem was the lack of a unified command structure with the mission being commanded by the Joint Chiefs of Staff in Washington.

The Holloway Commission recommended the establishment of a Joint Special Operations Command (JSOC) responsible for co-ordinating the special forces (SF) units from the Army, Air Force and Navy under a unified command. The commission also recommended that both the Army and Air Force be equipped with dedicated special operations aircraft and helicopters designed for night-time, long-range, low-level, covert, all-weather operations.

The US Special Operations Command (USSOC) based at MacDill Air Force Base, Florida was activated on 6 April 1987 with approximately 40,000 active, reserve and National Guard forces of the Army, Navy and Air Force.

Headquarters, Joint Special Operations Command based at Fort Bragg, North Carolina, is governed by USSOC. JSOC is responsible for overseeing matters pertaining to joint special operations and missions. This includes studying joint special operations requirements and techniques, ensuring interoperability and equipment standardisation, planning and conducting joint special operations exercises and training, and developing joint operational tactics. USSOC also provides personnel to establish Theatre Special Operations Command (TSOC) units. Each operational theatre has a separate command to meet its special operations requirements. These TSOC units plan, prepare, command and control Army, Navy and Air Force special operations forces (SOF) on behalf of regional combatant commanders and ensure that SOF missions are fully synchronised with conventional military operations. The TSOC provides a clear chain of command for in-theatre SOFs as well as trained staff to plan, conduct and support joint special operations missions. TSOC personnel also ensure that SOF personnel participate in theatre mission planning and that other theatre component commanders are familiar with all their operational and support requirements and capabilities.

The other major commands under USSOC are: US Army Special Operations Command (Airborne) based at Fort Bragg, North Carolina, Naval Special Warfare Command, based at Coronado, California and US Air Force Special Operations Command based at Hurlburt Field, Florida.

CHAPTER 1
US Army Special Operations Command (Airborne)

The US Army Special Operations Command (USASOC) was established at Fort Bragg, North Carolina on 1 December 1989 to enhance the readiness of Army special forces. This change streamlined the command and control of US Army special forces within USSOC. The Army's USSOC component provides special forces including Delta Force, Rangers, Special Operations Aviation, Psychological Operations and Civil Affairs forces for deployment as required around the world.

USASOC major subordinate commands include the US Army Special Forces Command (Airborne), US Army Civil Affairs and Psychological Operations Command (Airborne) and the US Army John F. Kennedy Special Warfare Center and School. Major subordinate units include 75th Ranger Regiment, 160th Special Operations Aviation Regiment (Airborne), and the US Army Special Operations Support Command (Airborne), which oversees the operations of the 528th Special Operations Support Battalion (Airborne) and the 12th Special Operations Signal Battalion (Airborne). USASOC commands both active Army and Reserve component SOF and provides National Guard special operations forces readiness, organisation and training.

US Army Special Forces

The mission of the USASOC is to train, validate and prepare Army special forces to undertake their various missions worldwide. There are five active special forces

Special forces soldiers seen during a *SPIES/FRIES* extraction by Black Hawk helicopter.

Special forces team seen firing M4 machine-guns equipped with M-230 grenade launchers.

groups and two reserve groups, each comprising around 1400 'Green Beret' soldiers organised into three battalions, a support company and a headquarters company. Each company is split into twelve-man 'A' Teams under the command of a captain. Each SF group is responsible for an area of the globe. These SF groups comprise:

1st Special Forces Group (Airborne), Fort Lewis, Washington, responsible for Pacific Command and Eastern Asia including Korea with a detachment based in Okinawa, Japan.

3rd Special Forces Group (Airborne), Fort Bragg, North Carolina, responsible for European Command to include Africa and Caribbean.

5th Special Forces Group (Airborne), Fort Campbell, Kentucky, responsible for Central Command to include south-west Asia, Kuwait central and north-east Africa.

7th Special Forces Group (Airborne), Fort Bragg, North Carolina, responsible for Southern Command including Central and South America, and Puerto Rico.

10th Special Forces Group (Airborne), Fort Carson, Colorado, responsible for European Command including north-west Asia with a Detachment 1st Battalion based in Germany.

There are two National Guard/Reserve Special Forces Groups:

19th Special Forces Group (Airborne), based at Camp Williams, Utah, responsible for Pacific Command including Asia.

20th Special Forces Group (Airborne), based at Birmingham, Alabama, responsible for Southern Command including Western Asia.

These special forces soldiers are carefully selected and schooled, including theatre specific training, to prepare them for their particular region of responsibility. They are trained to take part in five specific types of missions, which all special forces soldiers undertake: unconventional warfare, direct action, special reconnaissance, foreign internal defence and counter-terrorism.

Unconventional Warfare

Unconventional warfare involves conducting a broad spectrum of military and paramilitary operations in enemy-held, enemy-controlled, or politically sensitive territory. This requires long-duration, indirect activities including guerrilla warfare and other offensive, low-

Special forces soldiers deploy by parachute static-line.

Special forces team HALO jumping from an MH-47 Chinook.

visibility, or clandestine operations. SF soldiers are also trained to organise, train, equip, support and instruct indigenous forces in varying degrees.

HALO jumping.

Direct Action

Soldiers are trained to seize, damage, or destroy a target, and capture or recover personnel or *matériel* in support of strategic/operational objectives, or conventional forces. This includes conducting raids, ambushes and direct assault actions, emplacing mines and other munitions, finding and designating or illuminating targets for precision guided munitions, support for cover and deception operations and conducting independent sabotage missions within enemy-held territory.

Special Reconnaissance

Soldiers are trained to verify, through observation or other collection methods, information concerning enemy capabilities, intentions and activities in support of strategic/operational objectives or conventional forces. These actions complement national and theatre level collection efforts and include target acquisition, area assessment and post-strike reconnaissance data.

Foreign Internal Defence

In this type of mission soldiers assist another government in any actions programme intended to free and protect its society from subversion, lawlessness and insurgency. This includes training, advising and assisting a host nation's military and paramilitary forces, plus fostering internal development of economic, social, political and military segments of a nation's structure. Recent years have seen special forces assisting friendly nations in their counter-drugs operations and the training of counter-drugs paramilitary and police forces throughout Latin and Central America.

Counter-terrorism

Soldiers are trained to pre-empt or resolve terrorist incidents and provide interagency activity using highly specialised skills. Personnel from 1st Special Forces

doctrine. The centre conducts a full range of survival, evasion, resistance and escape training courses for SF soldiers as well as developing doctrine and new equipment for Army special operations.

To be selected for the special forces, potential candidates need to be above-average soldiers, to have obtained secret clearances and must have completed Basic Airborne Training. Having qualified, potential students attend the JFKSWCS for their selection course, which is conducted by 1st Battalion (JFKSWCS). Special forces soldiers undertake over two years' training to become qualified starting with the Basic Qualification Course, the Basic Military Foreign Language Qualification, followed by the Advance Skills Qualification.

The 1st Battalion is responsible for the selection course plus the special forces Weapons, Medical, Communications, Engineer and Officer Basic Qualification Courses. Selection comprises a three-week course designed to assess a student's physical and mental endurance whilst under pressure. Once students have successfully completed selection they move to the Basic Special Forces Qualification Course.

Students then move to the 3rd Battalion, responsible for basic military foreign language courses and also home to Civil Affairs, psychological operations and regional studies. Having completed this phase special forces students move to the 2nd Battalion for Advance Skills training. This includes:

Military Freefall Parachute Course. (This includes both HALO (High Altitude Low Opening) and HAHO (High Altitude High Opening) techniques jumping by day and by night. This includes a standard four-week military freefall course plus a three-week military freefall jumpmaster course.)

Anti-Terrorist Instructors Course (nine days)

Individual Terrorism Awareness Course (five days)

Survival, Evasion, Resistance and Escape Course (nineteen days)

Special Operations Target Interdiction (Snipers) Course (six weeks)

United Nations Peace-keeper's Operations Course (ten days)

Combat Diver Course

The basic Combat Diver Qualification conducted at Key West, Florida comprises a four-week course. There is also a Combat Diver Supervisor Course to qualify divers to supervise any military diving operations, and a Special Forces Medical Technician Course lasting three weeks.

During their entire training programme special forces soldiers are continually coached in medical, foreign language and academic skills. Once assigned to their specific Special Operations Group soldiers undertake

Army special forces personnel use the ram-air square parachute during HALO/HAHO jumps.

Operational Detachment-Delta (SFOD-D) are also used in these counter-terrorist missions.

Army Special Forces Selection/Training

To conduct these types of missions USASOC requires highly motivated and trained soldiers. Army special forces selection and training is undertaken at the US Army John F. Kennedy Special Warfare Center and School (JFKSWCS) based at Fort Bragg. The centre is responsible for special operations training, leadership development and

area-orientated specialised training for their mission and operational environment. Special forces soldiers are regularly deployed around the world undertaking a variety of roles including humanitarian and peace-keeping missions as well as counter-narcotic and other less publicised roles both at home and abroad.

Army special forces soldiers train as combat divers and undertake water operations including small boat operations, as seen here where they are deploying aboard a Chinook.

1st Special Forces Operational Detachment-Delta (SFOD-D)

Delta Force was formed on 19 November 1977 by Colonel C.A. Beckwith and is the US Army's special operations 'black' or clandestine unit, trained in hostage rescue, counter-terrorism and other highly specialised missions. Based on the UK's 22nd Special Air Service (22 SAS) Delta is split into three operational squadrons, A, B and C,

comprising 150 soldiers each, which in turn are split into troops. Stationed at Fort Bragg, Delta Force comprises volunteers taken mainly from other special operations and airborne units including the 'Green Berets', 75th Ranger Regiment, 82nd Airborne Division.

In recent years Delta Force has been moving increasingly away from 'green-army' missions, concentrating on counter-revolutionary warfare/counter-terrorist activities, although in August 1993 elements were deployed alongside 75th Ranger Regiment soldiers in Somalia during Operation *UNOSOM II* as part of Task Force Ranger.

ABOVE: An MH-47E Chinook from 160th SOAR deploys an Army special forces team by boat.

BELOW: As well as deploying special forces teams by Zodiac boat an MH-47E Chinook from 160th SOAR can also recover the team during a water landing.

The Zodiac drives into the Chinook in a flurry of spray.

Although never publicised, it was reported that their main mission was to find and capture the Somalian rebel leaders including Mohammad Farad Aidid. They also undertook this role during Operation *Just Cause* in Panama, resulting in the successful arrest of General Manuel Noriega. Delta Force troops were also involved in Operation *Desert Storm*, helping to locate Scud missile launchers and planning missions to locate and capture Saddam Hussein. They have also been actively involved in the location and capture of Bosnian war crime suspects.

Delta Force regularly works alongside other specialist units such as the UK's 22 SAS, the German GSG9 (*Grenzschutzgruppen*) and the French GIGN (*Group d'Intervention Gendarmerie Nationale*) plus other government agencies. Delta Force also provides a presence at US Embassies worldwide.

Army special forces are equipped with the latest radios and equipment and train for all terrain including tropical swamps.

A special forces soldier wearing protective headgear and armed with an M-4 rifle with M-230 grenade launcher and laser sighting system, prepares to storm a building during Military Operations in Urban Terrain (MOUT) training.

Special forces soldiers training at Fort Bragg seen undertaking fast-rope drills from a Black Hawk helicopter.

Demolition and working with explosives is an important part of the training syllabus at JFKSWCS.

ABOVE: Special forces soldiers train to fight in every climatic environment. This special forces soldier is seen operating a mortar in the Kuwait desert during a recent training exercise.

BELOW: Advance skills training for Army special forces soldiers includes the Combat Divers course at the Underwater Operations School based at Key West, Florida.

This soldier is Ranger, Airborne and special forces trained and is now passing his knowledge on as an instructor at Ranger School.

Rappelling skills are a requirement for special forces soldiers.

CHAPTER 2
Airborne School/Pathfinder School

All US Army special forces soldiers, US Navy SEALs and US Air Force special tactics personnel must be airborne-qualified. This training is conducted at Fort Benning, Georgia by the 1st Battalion (Airborne), 507th Infantry Regiment. This unit is also responsible for running the Pathfinder School, which trains soldiers to provide ground support for aircraft and helicopters operating from tactical Landing and Drop Zones (LZs/DZs).

Airborne School

Annually over 15,000 soldiers attend the US Army Basic Airborne School run by a cadre of US Army, US Marine Corps and US Air Force 'Black Hat' instructors. Their title comes from their distinctive black caps. The primary role of the Airborne School is to train a soldier in military parachute operations and to help develop mental and physical well-being. All students are volunteers and need to meet a basic standard, which includes being less than thirty-six years of age and passing a basic physical fitness test.

The school is split into six companies with a main head-quarter and headquarter company for administration plus four line companies. There is also a separate company, which provides parachute-rigging support to the school. Each company has a platoon and section sergeants plus squad leaders who remain with their students throughout the course.

The Basic Airborne Course lasts for three weeks,

A 'Black Hat' instructor gets to grips with a student during basic Ground-training week on how to land properly.

During week two students move onto the suspended harness and
Swing Landing Trainers (SLTs).

OPPOSITE: Much of the basic training involves teaching students to land
and roll safely. Here a female instructor is about to provide a few
helpful tips to a student.

Week two sees students using the 34-foot tower, Lateral Drift Apparatus (LDA) and mock door, learning how to exit an aircraft with other paratroopers, known as the 'mass exit' approach.

The LDA is used to instil confidence and teach students how to hit the ground sideways or backwards.

Working as a team, students prepare a parachute for the 250-foot Tower Jump.

OPPOSITE: A student hangs from the tower ring waiting for a 'Black Hat' instructor to give the order to release.

separated into Ground, Tower and Jump weeks culminating in five parachute jumps including a night jump. Throughout the course great emphasis is placed on physical fitness training and high standards of dress and appearance. This is one of the US Army's premier soldier self-confidence courses, designed to develop leadership, courage and mental and physical improvement. Not all students ultimately head for airborne or special forces units. Those who remain qualified wear an additional star emblem above their parachute wings.

Ground Training Week

This week is taken up with physical fitness and basic ground training, teaching students how to land safely and other basic airborne skills. This includes using the 34-ft tower and Lateral Drift Trainer (LDT) and how to line up and exit an aircraft door. At the end of this week students need to have qualified successfully on the 34-ft tower and show they can land safely using the LDT.

Tower Week

Tower week is devoted to enhancing the skills learned the previous week but now concentrating on the 'mass exit' approach using the 34-ft tower, the Swing Landing Trainer (SLT) and suspended harness apparatus. This training also includes learning how to line up and 'mass exit' an

aircraft in a stick. Once these basics have been learned students then move on to the famous 250-ft parachute towers, which dominate the Fort Benning skyline. Each tower has a parachute ring in each of the four quadrants of the compass. The wind direction will determine which ring will be used. Originally designed as a show-/fair-ground attraction in the late 1930s, the system was purchased by the Army and adapted to make an excellent parachute trainer. Other countries including the UK rely on using balloons for this phase of training. The system uses a simple electric motor to winch-up a student already strapped to his parachute, which is already open-linked to the ring. Once a safety line has been released the parachute is set free allowing the student to descend to the ground. As each student lands the ring is lowered to allow another student to be attached. Having mastered this phase students move on to their final Jump week.

Jump Week

Students need to complete five parachute jumps from an aircraft during this final week including one night jump using the standard US military T10 parachute. These jumps are normally held at Fryar Drop Zone at Fort Benning and conducted between Monday and Wednesday, allowing a run-over day of Thursday should any of the jumps be cancelled due to poor weather. The Graduation Ceremony is held on Friday at 11 a.m. at Eubanks Field on the Airborne Walk and parachute wings are awarded to successful students.

Students rig-up and prepare to board their USAF transport aircraft at Lawson Army Airfield, located on Fort Benning, for the short flight to Fryar Drop Zone. Students can either jump from a USAF C-130 Hercules or the new C-17 Globemaster III. The C-17, which has recently entered service with the USAF, has become a firm

OPPOSITE: 'Black Hat' instructors give advice to a student during his descent from the tower onto a specially prepared sand landing area.

BELOW: During Jump week students walk to their USAF C-130H transport at Lawson Army Airfield for their first parachute jump.

An instructor 'jump master' checks a student's parachute and harness in the hangar at Lawson Army Airfield prior to his first jump.

Equipped with white static-lines these students make their first
parachute jump from a USAF C-17 Globemaster.

OPPOSITE: Students depart a C-17 Globemaster at Fryar Drop Zone,
Fort Benning on their first of five parachute jumps.

favourite for paratroopers with its spacious cargo hold and large step on the para-door. Due to the increased fuselage turbulence an extra 5 ft has been added to the standard parachute static-line. Normal US Army parachute static-lines are 15 ft in length and colour-coded yellow. The new 20-ft static-line for the C-17 is colour-coded white, easily identifying students who are destined for this aircraft. Within the next few years an adjustable static-line will be in service allowing only one type to be used. Presently if the C-17 is unserviceable all the parachutes fitted with the white static-line need to be re-packed and fitted with a yellow static-line.

Students parachute jump at 1250 ft and prior to each jump a 'wind-checker' parachutes to test the drift rate. The next pass will see the students depart the aircraft and they must all be on the ground before the next aircraft enters the Drop Zone (DZ). One of the features of the new C-17 Globemaster is that the aircraft can conduct a Computer-Controlled Air Drop (CCAD). This is one of the main features of the new aircraft and once the pilot has logged the DZ grids and height for the jump into the navigational computer the system takes over and flies the entire circuit, approach and drop automatically. This includes calculating wind drift and other variables and initiating the red and green-to-go jump lights.

The US Navy SEALs attend this course at the end of their SEAL training period before moving on to the military freefall course. Other special forces and 75th Ranger Regiment troops all need to be fully jump-qualified to remain operational.

Pathfinder Course

The 1st Battalion (Airborne), 507th Infantry Regiment/ Airborne School is also responsible for running the three-week Pathfinder Course. This course provides selected special operations and airborne soldiers with the skills to

OPPOSITE: Pathfinders deploy onto Fryar Drop Zone, from a UH-60 Black Hawk helicopter which has been guided into the area by a student Pathfinder running the LZ.

BELOW: 75th Ranger Regiment 'jump master' gives the signal for a Pathfinder to leave the Black Hawk helicopter during the Pathfinder Course at Fort Benning.

support air assault and airdrop operations. The course qualifies students to: select, establish and operate suitable Helicopter Landing Sites (HLS) and parachute DZs by day or night; provide limited air traffic control and navigational assistance to rotor and fixed-wing operations; conduct and manage underslung load operations from an HLS; and manage loads and troops at either an HLS or parachute DZ. They are also trained to provide limited weather observations to USAF and Army helicopters. The course also trains students in ground navigation and the various methods of getting into theatre either on foot or by parachute, helicopter fast-rope, by vehicle or by boat. Much of the training concentrates on the use of ground-to-air communications and the correct establishment and operation of a DZ with aircraft operating either a Computer-Controlled Drop System (CCDS) or Ground Marker Release System (GMRS). The GMRS is where the pilot releases his load on visual cues to VS17 panels set out on the ground in a pre-designated code either using a letter or pattern, or following verbal directions by VHF/UHF radio from the Pathfinder on the ground. Students complete the course at Fort Benning with a three-day field exercise, which includes running both a DZ and an HLS, and conducting sling-load operations with helicopters as part of a Pathfinder team. This can either be as a team leader or assistant team leader, both of which are graded positions.

ABOVE: 'Black Hat' Instructors patrol the DZ, shouting advice to students as they descend to the ground at Fort Benning.

OPPOSITE: Jumping in sticks of three, paratroopers leave a Black Hawk helicopter under guidance from a student Pathfinder operating the LZ at Fryar Drop Zone.

CHAPTER 3
US Ranger Training Brigade/ Long Range Surveillance Leaders Course

The US Army Ranger Training Brigade is responsible for the selection and training of US Army Rangers, as well as running the US Army Long Range Surveillance Leaders Course (LRSLC).

Ranger Training Brigade

The US Army Rangers have a long history with their origins going as far back as the early seventeenth century when small units of American colonists were engaged to fight the Indians using the same woodsman skills and tactics as the Indians. This emphasis on self-reliance, tactics and soldier skills remains an important part of today's Ranger training.

Attaining a Ranger tab is an important step in the career of any soldier and is not easily achieved. Only around 30 per cent of a class will graduate without repeating a phase, but eventually 52 per cent will pass the course and are awarded their Ranger tabs, which is 3 per cent of the entire US Army. The Ranger course is open to officer and enlisted volunteers who are eligible for assignment to units whose primary mission is to engage in close-combat, direct-fire battle. Ranger School is designed for those who require mission-specific special skills and offers up to seven officer and seven enlisted specialities, as well as certain specialities to sister service units and foreign volunteers. Graduates return to their various units to pass on their new skills. There is much confusion between the US Army Rangers and the 75th Ranger Regiment. Not all Rangers are part of the 75th Ranger Regiment although officers and enlisted soldiers from the 75th Ranger Regiment, who are part of US Army Special Operations Command, need to graduate from Ranger School during their time with the unit. Most Ranger students have completed Basic Airborne Training before attending Ranger School.

Ranger training is an arduous course undertaken in three phases at three locations: 4th Ranger Training Battalion, Camp Rogers at Fort Benning, Georgia; 5th Ranger Training Battalion based at Camp Merrill near Dahlonega, Georgia and 6th Ranger Training Battalion based at Camp James E. Rudder, Florida. The course lasts for sixty-one days with around forty days operating in field conditions.

Entrance to Camp Frank D. Merrill, named after General Merrill and his 'Merrill's Marauders', who operated in Burma during World War II.

Phase 1: Camp Rogers, Fort Benning
This first phase is designed to weed out the soldiers who have not physically or mentally prepared for the course while introducing them to the basics of combat patrolling. The first week of the course, known as the Ranger Assessment Phase (RAP) week, places heavy emphasis on physical fitness tests with students undertaking the Army Physical Readiness Test, the Combat Water Survival Test, water confidence tests, a five-mile run, a buddy run with obstacle course, instruction in hand-to-hand combat and rifle-bayonet fighting techniques, and a refresher

Camp Merrill is situated in the Chattahoochee National Forest and home to 5th Training Battalion and the Mountain Training Phase.

parachute jump. Soldier skills are taught and students are instructed in combat patrols, navigation, the fundamentals of the ambush, reconnaissance patrols, and basic field craft. RAP week concludes with a sixteen-mile foot march to Camp Darby, where students complete the famed Darby Queen obstacle course, and then apply the fundamentals of conducting ambush and reconnaissance patrols in a field environment at squad level. This phase helps develop military skills, leadership, stamina and to build teamwork spirit with other students. It is at this stage that the majority of students dropped from the course are identified, having failed to meet a course prerequisite for graduation, voluntarily quit, or are injured. After successfully completing this phase students move on to the 5th Ranger Training Battalion for the Mountain Phase.

Phase 2: Mountain Phase – Camp Merrill

Camp Merrill is located fifty miles north of Atlanta, Georgia on the southern edge of the Appalachian chain's Blue Ridge Mountains in the Chattahoochee National Forest close to the town of Dahlonega. During this phase students receive instruction in military rock climbing, which includes knots, belays, bridge construction, rappelling and climbing techniques. This phase includes a two-day field exercise at Yonah. Students also receive instruction on how to conduct an ambush and raid at platoon level. Students then spend the remainder of this phase executing raid and ambush patrols throughout the Chattahoochee National Forest. These patrols are conducted in mountainous terrain, making living, operations and navigating difficult. Students, who have no rank insignia, take turns to plan and lead a patrol with a variety of mission tasks including covert reconnaissance, ambush and escape and evade. Ranger cadre instructors continually monitor each patrol and safety is of prime concern with a Medical Black Hawk UH-60A on permanent standby based at Camp Merrill.

This stage of training ends with a four- and five-day field training exercise, which includes an air assault phase. These field-training exercises require students to conduct a variety of missions day and night against an opposing force. Each day a patrol is given a separate task/mission to complete, usually requiring a long march to reach the objective or an air assault to a designated landing site, followed by a march over difficult mountainous terrain to reach the objective and finally a night march to a

A Ranger student plans a mission in the woods during the Mountain Training Phase.

helicopter pick-up point. Each phase requires accurate navigation and time-on-target to successfully complete the mission. An instructor will select a student at random to be mission leader. Even when weary, hungry and not having slept for several days the student patrol leader will need to plan the mission and motivate his patrol over a twenty-four hour period.

Students who fail to complete their missions successfully can be backdated to start again with the next intake. Those who quit are returned to unit (RTU). Students who complete this phase are driven to Dobbins Air Force Base, north of Atlanta, and undertake an airborne parachute insertion into the next and final phase.

Phase 3: Swamp/Jungle Phase – Florida

The final phase takes place at Camp James E. Rudder located at Eglin Air Force Base, Florida. Students are taught how to undertake small unit amphibious operations including the use of Zodiac boats as well as operating in a swamp and jungle environment. They learn how to successfully undertake small raids and ambushes in this unique environment. Upon arrival at the 6th Ranger Training Battalion, students receive classroom training on reptiles indigenous to the environment, equipment waterproofing, survival, and movement and patrolling techniques for this type of terrain. The phase ends with a tenday field exercise including a parachute assault followed by a series of air assaults, raids and ambushes. At the end of the course those students who have successfully met the course graduation requirements parachute back into Fort Benning to receive their coveted Ranger tab.

The Ranger tab is not easily earned and graduation standards remain high. Rangers have proved their ability to overcome mental and physical challenges and shown their capability at mastering small-arms field skills and planning and leading small-unit patrols in difficult operational environments to accomplish a variety of combat missions. A Ranger's experience goes back with him to his regular unit to be passed on and help improve the overall combat skills of the US Army.

ABOVE: A Ranger student makes an inventory of his patrol's equipment at a forest resting point during a day-into-night ambush mission.

BELOW: Ranger students are equipped with a variety of Night Vision Goggles (NVGs) to conduct their night raids and ambushes.

ABOVE: During their training phase Ranger students conduct several parachute assaults.

OPPOSITE: Equipped with a Squad Automatic Weapon (SAW), this Ranger student, having spent several days patrolling in the woods near Dahlonega, sets off for another patrol and ambush mission. He has had little sleep for several days.

Long Range Surveillance Leaders Course

This thirty-three day course is run by D Company, 4th Ranger Training Battalion at Camp Rogers, Fort Benning, Georgia. Today's Long Range Surveillance Units are linked to the Long Range Surveillance Patrols (LRSPs) which achieved distinction for their scouting skills during the Vietnam War. Today's LRSUs are tasked with providing passive reconnaissance and intelligence-gathering attached to either an Army Division or Corps as well as at Regiment level. Usually operating in six-man teams, LRSUs are trained to deploy up to 150 miles and for up to thirty days behind enemy lines. They can be deployed either by aircraft (HAHO/HALO), helicopter (Special Patrol Insertion and Extraction System – SPIES – or Fast Rope), small boat,

by vehicle or on foot. They are not intended as direct action teams (this is the role of Army Rangers or special forces 'A' Teams), but to use covert skills to obtain strategic and tactical intelligence on enemy activity and disposition. They provide bomb damage assessments, terminal guidance using laser designators and other means to destroy enemy targets. They also provide fire control for artillery missions as well as locating enemy strength and dispositions.

The Long Range Surveillance Leaders Course (LRSLC) is extremely demanding with students working sixteen hours per day, seven days per week. Training concentrates on the use of secure speech radios (HF/VHF/UHF), land navigation, intelligence gathering, imagery, survival, vehicle identification, escape and evade techniques, mission planning, the use of hide sites and other forms of covert observation, plus specialist insertion and extraction techniques along with air assault and airborne skills. LRSU techniques are also used by reconnaissance platoons attached to each of the three 75th Ranger Regiment battalions. Graduates of the course return to their units with the skills to conduct reconnaissance and surveillance missions.

The Flight Support Branch Detachment of 1st/11th Infantry Regiment known as the Ravens forms an important part of the training programme at Fort Benning and is involved in supporting Ranger, Pathfinder and LRSLC training as well as the US Army Infantry School, Infantry Training Brigade, School of the Americas and other units based at Fort Benning. Based at Lawson Army Air Field, the Flight operates six Sikorsky UH-60A Black Hawks with thirteen pilots and twenty-six crew chiefs plus engineers. The Ravens fly over thirty hours per month and deploy regularly to Camp Merrill and Camp James E. Rudder to support Ranger training, as well as supporting LRSLC missions. They also provide training support to the Pathfinder School, undertaking day/night underslung load lifting and parachute dropping to DZs operated by Pathfinder students.

Supporting the various Ranger training missions requires specialist-training skills for the pilots who need to transport eleven fully equipped Rangers, each weighing around 260 lb, into and out of small helicopter pick-up and landing zones during both day and night flying conditions. Pilots rely on the use of Night Vision Goggles (NVGs) to accomplish their training during the hours of limited visibility. The Flight also provides support during LRSLC training to students undertaking instruction in the Special Patrol Insertion/Extraction System and Fast Rope Insertion/Extraction System, known as SPIES and FRIES. This training is then used to insert and extract LRSLC students during their cadre-led and student graded field training exercises.

OPPOSITE: Long Range Reconnaissance Patrol students are instructed on methods of entry into theatre including fast-roping.

ABOVE: Long Range Recon Patrol personnel being hauled out of the woods using the SPIES and FRIES technique.

OPPOSITE: Students on the LRSLC prepare their equipment prior to being deployed into theatre by Black Hawk helicopter.

ABOVE: LRSLC students learning how to fast-rope at Fort Benning.

An LRSLC instructor from D Co., 4th Ranger Training Battalion at Camp
Rogers watches over a student during SPIES and FRIES training.

A UH-60 Black Hawk lands in a small clearing in the woods to deploy a Ranger Patrol for a day-into-night patrol and raid.

ABOVE: Heliborne assaults are an important part of Ranger training.

BELOW: A UH-60 Black Hawk pilot manoeuvring into position to deploy a Ranger patrol into the forest near Dahlonega.

OPPOSITE: A Black Hawk pilot from Fort Benning flying in support of Ranger training and LRSLC missions.

CHAPTER 4
75th Ranger Regiment (Airborne)

The 75th Ranger Regiment is part of the United States Army Special Operations Command and is the premier rapid deployment light infantry unit. The Army maintains the regiment at a high level of readiness and each battalion can deploy anywhere in the world within eleven hours. The regiment led the way in October 1983 during Operation *Urgent Fury* in Grenada, when the 1st and 2nd Battalions conducted an airborne assault on Point Salines airfield and helped to rescue American students. All three battalions were deployed to Panama in December 1989 during Operation *Just Cause*. They conducted airborne assaults onto Omar Torrijos International Airfield and secured entry for the 82nd Airborne Division, as well as conducting airborne assaults onto Rio Hato airfield and follow-on operations. In 1991 elements of the regiment were deployed on Operation *Desert Storm* along with other US special operations units and conducted deep-strike raids against enemy communications and assisted in patrolling behind enemy lines searching for Scud missile launchers.

In 1993 elements of 3rd Battalion deployed to Mogadishu, Somalia as part of Task Force Ranger along with Delta Force and 160th Special Operations Aviation Regiment (Airborne) to support Operation *UNOSOM II*. The Rangers captured several enemy leaders responsible

75th Ranger Regiment operates a fleet of British-made Land Rovers known as Ranger Special Operations Vehicles (RSOVs) used as gunships, command and control vehicles or as ambulances.

for launching attacks on United Nations forces. During this deployment Rangers conducted a daring eighteen-hour daylight rescue mission, which successfully recovered a patrol cut off in Mogadishu, which resulted in the downing of several 160th SOAR, MH-60L Black Hawks and the deaths of six Rangers.

The 75th Ranger Regiment is composed of three Ranger battalions, 1st Battalion based at Hunter Army Air Field, Georgia, 2nd Battalion at Fort Lewis, Washington and 3rd Battalion and Regiment Headquarters at Fort Benning, Georgia. The primary task of the regiment is to plan and conduct special missions in support of US policy and objectives. This includes infiltration and exfiltration by land, sea and air. The regiment is also tasked to conduct direct action operations and raids, to recover personnel and special equipment and to conduct conventional or special light missions. Rangers train for theatre entry operations, securing entry points for follow-on forces. They are equipped to sustain these operations for a period of thirty days prior to the arrival of follow-on forces. This type of mission includes airfield seizures and

LEFT: This Ranger is a qualified paratrooper with star to denote he is current, HALO/HAHO- and Pathfinder- and marksman-trained.

BELOW: 75th Ranger Regiment troops parachuting from a C-17 Globemaster.

A 75th Ranger Regiment massed parachute jump at Fort Benning in July 2001. In October they undertook a night parachute assault and raid into Afghanistan.

deep-strike raids using air assault, airborne and Tactical Air Land Operations (TALO) as well as working alongside other special operations units.

Each Ranger battalion comprises 580 personnel assigned to three rifle companies plus a headquarters company. Each rifle company comprises 152 Rangers with the remainder assigned to headquarters company. As light infantry units Rangers battalions have only a few specialised vehicles and crew-served weapons systems, which include modified Land Rovers known as Ranger Special Operations Vehicles (RSOVs) equipped either as command and control vehicles, medical ambulances or armed with .50 calibre machine-gun.

All personnel are volunteers and must meet the same physical and mental criteria. All officers and NCOs must be airborne- and Ranger-qualified prior to volunteering. Enlisted soldiers can attend Airborne and Ranger School once they have been accepted. Once accepted into the 75th Ranger Regiment officers and NCOs complete the Ranger Orientation programme to familiarise themselves with regimental policies, standard operating procedures (SOPs) and Ranger standards. Enlisted soldiers complete the Ranger Indoctrination programme to assess their physical qualifications and to be instructed in basic regimental standards. Failure to pass these programmes is justification to return soldiers to their home units. Enlisted soldiers who are not Ranger-qualified attend a course to prepare them for their time at Ranger School.

Each Ranger battalion has a reconnaissance platoon to undertake long-range reconnaissance and prepare for the arrival of the battalion. The regiment works alongside other special operations aviation units such as the 160th Special Operations Aviation Regiment (Airborne) and US Air Force Special Operations Command including their Sikorsky MH-53M Pave Low IV helicopters, MC-130 Combat Talon IIs, Combat Shadow aircraft and the AC-130

A 75th Ranger departs the drop zone with a Stinger missile system.

A 75th Ranger signals his team as others clear the drop zone during a rare daylight parachute assault. The 75th Ranger Regiment conducts its assaults at night.

The shoulder patch of the 1st Battalion, 75th Ranger Regiment.

Spectre gunship. The majority of training is undertaken at night to reflect their operational roles and Rangers undertake their airborne and heliborne assaults almost exclusively at night. Every member of the 75th Ranger Regiment has his own NVGs. Their weapons, including the special operations Colt M4, are equipped with NVG sighting systems and laser-lights. The regiment relies heavily on external fire support and works regularly with naval gunfire support, artillery units, AC-130 Spectre gunships and the 160th SOARs, MH-6 Little Birds and the MH-60L Direct Action Penetrator Black Hawk. Rangers are also equipped with M4 and M240 machine-guns, the M249 Squad Automatic Weapon (SAW), 0.50 in calibre machine-guns, the 84 mm Ranger anti-tank weapon and the Stinger anti-aircraft missile system.

75th Ranger Regiment troops assault an airfield equipped with 0.50-in-machine-gun-armed RSOVs. 75th Rangers train for theatre entry and raiding missions.

Above: Rangers fast-rope from a 160th SOAR MH-47D during a daylight rehearsal for a night raiding mission.

Right: A Ranger armed with an M4 carbine equipped with laser and optic sighting system.

Rangers are lightly equipped for their special operations role and are equipped with the 84 mm Ranger Anti-tank Weapon System (RAWS). These Rangers are undertaking Military Operations in Urban Terrain (MOUT) training and are equipped with NVGs.

ABOVE: Rangers are deployed aboard a 160th SOAR MH-6 Little Bird during a training mission.

RIGHT: Rangers, like other special forces, use the latest equipment including secure speech radios.

Rangers equipped with M4 carbines patrolling a swamp in Florida.

CHAPTER 5
160th Special Operations Aviation Regiment (Airborne)

The 160th Special Operations Aviation Regiment (Airborne) – SOAR – provides aviation support to Army special operations forces. The regiment consists of modified MH-6 Little Birds, MH-60L/K Black Hawks and MH-47D/E Chinooks. After the failed Operation *Eagle Claw* mission, the Army formed a special aviation unit to support special operations. This comprised modified Army helicopters flown by the best and most experienced Army aviators from 101st Airborne Division and concentrated on low-level night operations. The unit, known as 160th Aviation Battalion, became operational on 16 October 1981. Because of the unit's constant attachments and detachments as it prepared for its missions, it became

RIGHT: MH-6 Little Birds and MH-60L Black Hawks on the flight line at Fort Campbell. The Black Hawks in the rear with folded blades are kept ready for instant deployment aboard USAF transports.

BELOW: A Boeing MH-47E Chinook departs for a night training mission.

The Boeing MH-47E Chinook is operated exclusively by 160th SOAR and is dedicated to long-range low-level covert missions in poor weather.

known as Task Force 160 and later 'The Night Stalkers' due to its focus on night operations. On 16 May 1990 the unit was reorganised and designated the 160th Special Operations Aviation Regiment (Airborne).

The regiment currently consists of four battalions based at Fort Campbell, Kentucky and Hunter Army Air Field, Georgia. These comprise:

1st/160th Fort Campbell: A/Company, MH-6 Little Birds; B/Company AH-6 Little Birds; C/Company, MH-60L/K/DAP Black Hawk; D/Company MH-60 Black Hawk; E/Company, Maintenance.

2nd/160th Fort Campbell: A/Company, MH-47E Chinook; B/Company, MH-47E Chinook; D/Company,

Maintenance.

3rd/160th Hunter AAF, Georgia: A/Company: MH60L/K/DAP Black Hawk; B/Company, MH-47D Chinook; D/Company, MH-60L/K/DAP Black Hawk; C/Company, Maintenance.

4th/160th Fort Campbell: Regimental Headquarters, A/B/C and Support Company plus Systems Integration and Management Office, and Special Operations Aviation Training Company. The Systems Integration and Management Office is responsible for validating and trials of new equipment for the 160th SOAR. Any new equipment must prove to enhance mission capability, show reliability and maintainability and be used throughout the fleet.

All members of the 160th SOAR, ground and aircrew, officers and enlisted soldiers, are volunteers and must complete Basic Mission Qualification (BMQ). The Officer

The 160th SOAR operates a fleet of AH/MH-6 Little Birds. The AH-6 Little Bird can be armed with a variety of weapons including rockets, seen here being loaded up, prior to a training mission.

A 160th SOAR AH-6 Little Bird launching a salvo of folding fin rockets.

Qualification Course lasts fourteen weeks while the enlisted Qualification Course is three weeks long.

Aircrew training includes 'Green Platoon', comprising twenty-three days of classroom and field training, use of personnel weapons, basic combat lifesaving certificate, close quarters combat training, land navigation, road marches, underwater escape training, travel security and legal matters prior to flying training. All aircrew are already experienced aviators and it takes a further six to ten years to become a flight leader. The training is in three phases: Basic Mission Qualified, which takes around two years, Fully Mission Qualified, which takes a further four years, and Flight Leader Qualified in around eight to ten years.

To become Basic Mission Qualified aviators need to undertake mission-specific training in aerial gunnery and shipboard operations. Mission-specific training is also conducted in various operational settings including from rigs, platforms, desert, jungle, mountain, urban and maritime settings. Personnel also undertake Joint Operations Training with other aviation units. Almost all these missions are undertaken at night using NVGs. The 160th SOAR has a 'train as you fight' mentality and has been involved in operations in Grenada, Panama, The Gulf and Somalia. The helicopters operated by the 160th SOAR have been specially developed to undertake long-range covert night operations and have been equipped with the latest mission systems to allow crews to use NVGs in almost all weather and operational environments.

Sikorsky MH-60L/K

The MH-60L and MH-60K are special operations variants of the standard US Army UH-60 Black Hawk. The MH-60L has up-rated engines, nose-mounted Forward-Looking Infra-Red (FLIR) and weather radar along with aircraft survivability equipment and secure speech radios. The MH-60K has an up-rated engine and full glass cockpit with an integrated avionics system compatible with the MH-47E Chinook. The MH-60K is shipboard capable and can be easily folded to go in a ship's hangar deck or air transported in C-5 or C-17 aircraft. FLIR and survivability equipment has increased the gross weight to 24,000 lb

ABOVE: The UH-60 Black Hawk can be transported in all USAF heavy transport aircraft, an important requirement for the 160th SOAR's fleet of MH-60L/K variants.

BELOW: An MH-47E Chinook departing after dropping off a patrol.

Sikorsky AH-60L Direct Action Penetrator

This is an armed variant of the UH-60L equipped with a thermal imaging system (FLIR) and nose-mounted radar along with survivability equipment and satellite communications. The UH-60L DAP is equipped with the ESS and day/night sighting systems and can be armed with a variety of weapons depending on the mission such as Hellfire missiles, 70 mm rocket pods, Stinger air-to-air missiles, grenade launchers and a selection of door and ESS-mounted 0.50 in machine-guns and 7.62 mm Miniguns. In the Close Air Support (CAS) role special forces and Rangers can use the UH-60L DAP to provide close-in precision ground-fire, working together with AC-130 Spectre and Spooky gunships to deliver accurate and devastating fire support even on the darkest of nights.

Boeing MH-6J Little Bird

The 160th SOAR has been operating specially developed versions of the US Army OH-6 Cayuse since 1981. These small, easily transportable Little Birds have been developed by the 160th SOAR into two variants: the AH-6, which can be armed, and a reconnaissance/forward air control and troop-carrying variant called the MH-6. They were the first Army helicopters into action during Operation *Urgent Fury* in Grenada in 1983. They have taken part in almost every military action undertaken by the US since 1982 and operate almost exclusively at night. They were operated in the Persian Gulf in 1987 when they attacked an Iranian gunboat, and also took part in Panama, Gulf War, Haiti and Somalia missions. The Little Birds have recently undergone an avionics update allowing the helicopters to be easily changed from AH to MH, designated MH-6Js. These helicopters are painted in infra-red-reflective black and have a fully defensive suite with infra-red jammers, satellite communications and an NVG-compatible cockpit. Avionics include a mission/flight management system, colour digital map, thermal imaging sighting system including FLIR, laser range finder, secure speech radios and a quick-change ordnance mounting system. Known as 'The Plank' this system can be used to carry four special forces soldiers on the outside of the fuselage with two inside or it can be armed with a variety of weapons. These include Hellfire missiles, Stinger missiles, 70 mm rockets and M134 Miniguns. The MH-6J has a 400 nm range and can be loaded and unloaded into a C-130 or C-5/C-17 transport aircraft in fewer that ten minutes. Twenty-two Little Birds can be loaded into a C-5 or twelve in a C-17. Future updates of the MH-6J Little Birds will see an up-rated engine, new six-blade main rotor and Full Authority Digital Engine Control (FADEC). Role equipment updates will also include improved night vision, communications

The 160th SOAR operates three variants of the Black Hawk, the MH-60L, MH-60K and armed AH-60L Direct Action Penetrator (DAP) using the Black Hawk's ESS system to carry a variety of guns, rockets and missiles.

(11,000 kg), 2000 lb (900 kg) heavier than a normal Army UH-60L. Two pilots fly the MH-60K with two gunners armed with 7.62 mm Miniguns or 0.50 in GECALs and the helicopter can carry twelve special forces troops. The mission radius is around 200 miles but using air-to-air refuelling and auxiliary fuel tanks fitted to the External Stores System (ESS) can extend this.

A 160th SOAR MH-6K Black Hawk operating in the desert during a Combat Search and Rescue (CSAR) training mission.

Equipped with nose-mounted radar and FLIR plus self-defence suite, the MH-60L Black Hawk is the workhorse of the 160th SOAR.

Pilots assigned to the 160th SOAR spend many years training including flying and operating in extreme environments including the desert.

ABOVE: An MH-47E Chinook lifts away at sunset with a pair of Hummer vehicles and steel ladder for the crew on a night mission.

BELOW: An MH-60K hooks up to a USAF MC-130P Combat Shadow tanker for an air-to-air refuel, just one of the missions undertaken at night.

and navigation systems plus an Integrated Flight/Mission/Weapons and Tactical Display System linked through a MIL-STD-1553 databus. There are also plans for a new lightweight 'Universal Plank' for weapons, fuel tanks, laser designators and personnel.

MH-47E Chinook

The 160th SOAR operates two special operations variants of the CH-47 Chinook, the MH-47 Delta and the MH-47 Echo. The MH-47D Chinook is a standard US Army CH-46D but with added special operations role equipment. This includes standard fuel tanks and cockpit but with added secure speech radios and satellite communications, updated navigation and avionics suite, thermal imaging and air-to-air refuel capability. This variant also has updated aircraft survivability equipment including radar and laser warning systems plus infra-red jammers and countermeasures.

The MH-47E Chinook was developed by Boeing specifically for the 160th SOAR. It was designed to be able to complete a five-and-a-half-hour covert mission over a 350 nm (556 km) radius at low level, day or night, in adverse weather over any type of terrain and to do so with a 90 per cent probability of success. The MH-47E has a fully integrated (glass cockpit) avionics system (IAS), which is compatible and interchangeable with the MH-60K. The IAS allows global communications. Navigation and weather penetration equipment includes FLIR and multi-mode terrain following/avoidance radar for nap-of-the-earth and low-level flight operations at night in adverse weather conditions. The MH-47E has twice the fuel capacity of the standard CH-47D, an aerial refuelling system, plus up-rated T55-L-714 engines with full authority digital engine management systems. The MH-47E can carry forty-four troops and special operations vehicles internally.

A flight of Black Hawks landing at a desert strip during a deployment to Egypt.

Armed with M134 Miniguns a pair of MH-60K Black Hawks and an MH-47E Chinook deploy a special forces raiding team.

ABOVE: Rangers fast-rope from a 160th SOAR MH-60L to storm a building during MOUT training.

BELOW: 75th Ranger Regiments are supported by 3rd/160th SOAR based at Hunter AAF alongside the 1st/75th Ranger Regiment.

CHAPTER 6
US Air Force Special Operations Command

With a history reaching back to the 'Air Commandos' and 'Carpetbaggers' of World War II, today's Air Force Special Operations Command continues in the tradition of 'quiet professionals' responsible for providing highly specialised air support to special forces wherever and whenever it is needed.

US Air Force Special Operations Command (AFSOC) has a headquarters at Hurlburt Field Air Force Base, Florida and became part of US Special Operations Command in April 1987. After several name changes and reorganisations in the mid-1990s, the US Air Force Special Operations Command is now split into three wings which in turn are divided into Operational Groups, each with a geographical area of responsibility.

Air Force Special Operations Command, Headquarters, Hurlburt Field, Florida,

16th Special Operations Wing (SOW), Hurlburt Field, Florida

352nd Special Operations Group (SOG), RAF Mildenhall, UK

353rd Special Operations Group, Kadena Air Base, Japan

720th Special Tactics Group, Hurlburt Field, Florida

18th Flight Test Squadron, Hurlburt Field, Florida

US Air Force Special Operations School, Hurlburt Field, Florida

193rd Special Operations Wing, Air National Guard, Harrisburg, Pennsylvania.

919th Special Operations Wing, Air Force Reserve, Duke Field, Florida

280th Special Operations Communications Squadron, Air National Guard, Dothan, Alabama.

The 16th SOW is responsible for covering Central Command, Joint Forces Command and Southern Command; 352nd SOG is accountable for European Command and 353rd SOG for Pacific Command. Each Special Operations Group is split into Flying Squadrons along with a Special Tactics Squadron, a Maintenance Squadron and an Operations Support Squadron.

AFSOC is responsible for providing highly trained aviators operating specialised helicopters and aircraft, along

The unit badge of the UK-based 352nd OSS.

7th SOS operates the MC-130H Combat Talon II.

The 352nd Maintenance Squadron looks after the UK-based MC-130H, MC-130P and MH-53 Pave Lows.

Talon parachute jump May 1999.

with special tactics and rescue specialists. AFSOC's mission is to undertake the covert insertion and extraction of special forces personnel and their equipment, direct action, unconventional warfare, special reconnaissance, foreign internal defence and providing counter-terrorism support to unified commanders worldwide. The core tasks for AFSOC are grouped into four main mission areas: forward presence and engagement; information operations; precision employment/strike; and special operations forces mobility. To fulfil these missions the group averages around 4700 flying hours per month.

AFSOC has been involved in almost every operational mission undertaken by the US over the past twenty years. These include: Operation *Urgent Fury*, in Grenada (1983); Operation *Just Cause*, Panama (1989); Operation *Desert Shield* and *Desert Storm*, Gulf War (1990); Operation *Provide Comfort*, Kurdistan (1991); Operation *Restore Hope*, Somalia (1992); Operation *Uphold Democracy*, Haiti (1994); Operation *Deliberate Force/Joint Endeavour*, Balkans (1995); Operation *Joint Guard*, Balkans (1997); and Operation *Allied Force*, Kosovo (1999), along with numerous other missions including unconventional and non-combatant evacuations (NEOs). Several NEOs have been performed in Africa including Operation *Assured Response*, the evacuation of 2100 US citizens from Monrovia, Liberia in 1996, and another NEO from Brazzaville, Congo. Operation *Silver Wake* was an NEO of 1000 civilians from Albania. AFSOC has also been heavily involved in humanitarian missions around the world including Operation *Provide Comfort* in Kurdistan in 1991 when 352nd SOG Talons and MH-53 Pave Lows deployed to Turkey during the huge Allied effort to help the Kurds.

352nd Special Operations Group

One of AFSOC's busiest units and typical of its Group structure is the 352nd SOG based at RAF Mildenhall, UK. This unit is the air component for special operations within the European Command (EUCOM) theatre spanning three continents and 91 countries, with an operational area of over 13 million square miles. It is under the operational control of Special Operations Command Europe (SOCEUR). The unit plans for and executes general war and contingency operations using advanced aircraft, tactics and aerial refuelling to infiltrate, exfiltrate and resupply special operations forces such as US Army Special Forces and US Navy SEAL members. The 352nd SOG, like other Air Force Special Operations Groups, continually trains for rapid deployment providing a tailored response to a variety of different military and humanitarian situations ranging from the rescue of a downed pilot to non-combatant evacuation operations. Like other Special

Unit patch of the MH-53M Pave Low-equipped 21st SOS.

Unit patch of the combat controllers and para-rescue personnel of the 321st STS based at RAF Mildenhall, Suffolk, UK.

Operations units the Air Force operates almost exclusively at night.

The 352nd SOG has six squadrons, a headquarters and:

7th Special Operations Squadron operating the MC-130H Combat Talon II

21st Special Operations Squadron operating the MH-53M Pave Low IV

67th Special Operations Squadron operating the MC-130P Combat Shadow

321st Special Tactics Squadron

352nd Maintenance Squadron operating MC-130s/ MH-53M Pave Lows

352nd Operations Support Command

Special Operations Aircraft

In the mid 1980s as a result of the lessons learned from the Holloway study into US special forces, the US Air Force began to develop its own special operations-capable aircraft and helicopters to undertake long-range covert, insertion, extraction and resupply missions at night to support US special forces. Having already spent many

years undertaking CSAR missions, which included using C-130 Hercules as air-refuelling platforms, the Air Force began to update these aircraft and helicopters for special operations. Today, AFSOC operates three specialised variants of the C-130 Hercules and the MH-53M Pave Low IV, a much improved variant of the famous Jolly Green Giant of the Vietnam War.

The AC-130H Spectre and AC-130U Spooky gunships are derivatives of the C-130 Hercules and operate in the CAS, air interdiction and force protection roles. Capable of undertaking an entire mission at night, the AC-130 can provide precision fire onto small target areas. It can offer close air support of troops in contact with the enemy, and conduct convoy escort and urban operations as undertaken in Mogadishu, Somalia. Air interdiction missions are undertaken against pre-planned targets or targets of opportunity and force-protection missions include air base defence and facility defence. Able to be air-refuelled from KC-135s and KC-10s, the AC-130s can remain over an operational area for some considerable time.

AC-130 Gunship

The AC-130H Spectre is armed with 40 mm cannons and

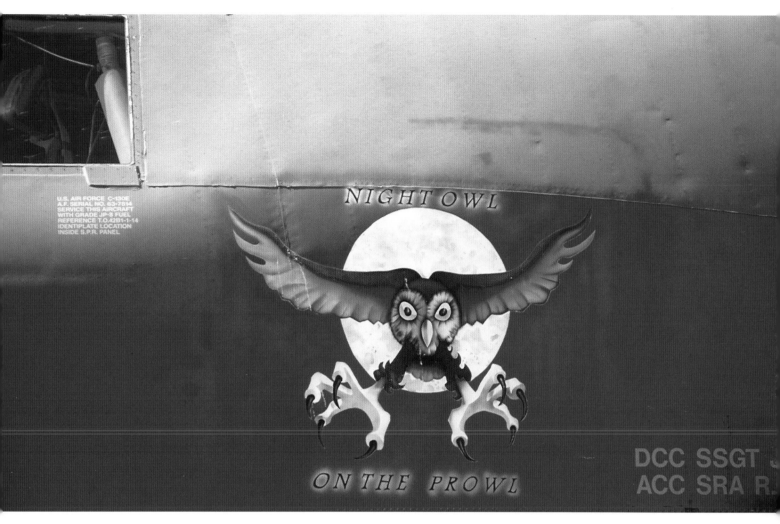

NIGHT OWL

ON THE PROWL

U.S. AIR FORCE C-130E
A.F. SERIAL NO. 63-7814
SERVICE THIS AIRCRAFT
WITH GRADE JP-8 FUEL
REFERENCE T.O.42B1-1-14
IDENTIPLATE LOCATION
INSIDE S.P.R. PANEL

DCC SSGT
ACC SRA R.

Combat artwork painted on the side of a UK-based MC-130P Combat Shadow operated by 67th SOS at RAF Mildenhall.

a 105 mm cannon. Its crew includes: pilot, co-pilot, navigator, fire control officer, electronic warfare officer, flight engineer, TV operator, infra-red detection set operator, loadmaster and four aerial gunners.

The AC-130U Spooky, known as the U-boat, is a pressurised variant of the Spectre and able to operate at higher altitudes. This variant is equipped with 40 mm cannon, 105 mm cannon and a 25 mm gun.

MC-130 Combat Talon II

The MC-130 Combat Talon II provides low-level, day, night and adverse weather capability in order to infiltrate, resupply and extract special forces. The Talon is equipped with inflight refuelling equipment, an inertial and global positioning satellite navigation system and a high-speed aerial delivery system. MC-130 Combat Talon crews are highly trained to undertake night missions and to make the best use of their aircraft systems. These include a combination of NVGs, terrain-following and avoidance radar, precision navigation, FLIR and electronic warfare systems, used to penetrate hostile airspace at low level in adverse weather conditions in order to locate small DZs and landing sites to deliver people and equipment at higher speeds. Low-level heavy drops of equipment can be carried out at speeds of 140 kt and precision delivery of light loads can be made at speeds of 250 kt. The Talon is also capable of conducting night, Self Contained Approaches (SCAs) and Departures, using Terrain Following/Terrain Avoidance (TF/TA) radar and precision navigation to fly down to a pre-designated glide path in adverse weather. Radar, NVGs and the FLIR system are then used to locate the runway and check that it is clear.

FOLLOWING PAGES: Special Tactics Squadron combat controllers and para-rescue men are amongst the most highly trained special forces personnel. They are seen here surrounded by some of their tactical and operational equipment.

A 21st SOS MH-53M Pave Low departs RAF Mildenhall for a day training mission.

The MH-53M Pave Low IV has one of the best-equipped cockpits including IDAS/MATT with four multi-function colour displays showing moving map, FLIR image, TF/TA radar and aircraft/mission information or any combination of these.

FOLLOWING PAGES: A 21st SOS MH-53M Pave Low IV on a training mission with two gunners armed with M134 Miniguns, and the tactics/flight engineer seen in the jump seat monitoring instruments, radios and defensive aid suites.

The rear-ramp gunner on a Pave Low can be armed with a 0.50 in gun or, as in this case, an M134 Minigun.

MC-130P Combat Shadow

The MC-130P Combat Shadow can undertake many of the Talon's missions but its primary role is night air-to-air refuelling of special operations helicopters. Crews wear NVGs and use the nose-mounted thermal imaging system to undertake low-level air-refuelling missions. These missions are undertaken in complete radio silence. A Combat Shadow can refuel two helicopters simultaneously using wing-mounted hoses and drogues. Secondary missions include the airdrop of small specialist teams, combat bundles and rubber raiding craft. NVG take-off and landing procedures can also be followed by the Combat Shadow.

EC-130 Commando Solo

This special operations variant of the C-130 Hercules is dedicated to psychological operations and civil affairs, broadcasting in AM, FM, high frequency, TV and military communications bands. Missions are flown at maximum altitude to ensure optimum propaganda patterns. These aircraft were used extensively in Panama and Serbia during Operations *Just Cause* and *Allied Force*.

MH-53M Pave Low IV

AFSOC operates a fleet of thirty recently updated MH-53M Pave Low helicopters. The Pave Low performs low-level, long-range day or night missions in adverse weather, for infiltration, exfiltration and resupply of special forces. With the recent transfer of the MH-60 Pave Hawk to Air Combat Command, the Pave Low is the only helicopter in the AFSOC inventory. The Pave Low is one of the most technologically advanced helicopters in use today,

A pair of Pave Lows arriving at a drop-off point.

using a combination of terrain-following/avoidance radar, FLIR, projected digital map display, NVGs and electronic warfare systems to operate in adverse weather conditions in hostile air space.

The helicopter is armour-plated and armed with three 7.62 mm Miniguns or a ramp-mounted .50 in machine-gun, and can transport thirty-eight troops or fourteen litters. It has a maximum capacity of 20,000 lb.

The MH-53M Pave Low IV has an upgraded cockpit with an Interactive Defence Avionics System/Multi-Mission Advanced Tactical Terminal (IDAS/MATT). This system integrates all the helicopter's mission, navigation and electronic warfare systems through a MIL-STD-1553 databus to provide electronic order of battle information, correlated onto a digital moving map for presentation on one of the colour Multi-Function Displays (MFDs). This puts all the tactical information onto a single screen, which can be updated inflight by satellite systems. This system

will display the helicopter's route, how this is affected by new threats and at what height to avoid detection. The system will also display an electronic image of the terrain outside which alters perspective as the height is changed. The system also displays the route being flown, the fuel burn and ETA. If a threat appears on the planned route the system will automatically work out the best alternate route and speed to fly, and still remain time-on-target. The system not only works out routes and threats but will also identify a threat and launch the appropriate countermeasures, which may be chaff or flares. This system will be fitted into the new special operations CV-22 Osprey.

Special Tactics Squadron

The para-rescue members, combat controllers and combat weathermen of the Special Tactics Squadrons are amongst the most highly trained special forces operatives. Special tactics personnel are skilled in air traffic control, terminal attack control, personnel recovery, combat trauma medical response, communications, forward weather observations, demolition, weapons and small unit tactics. Both para-rescue members (PJs) and combat control team personnel (CCTs) undertake a demanding selection course lasting eighteen months for PJs and fourteen months for CCTs.

The course comprises an Initial Qualification Training Course (IQTC). This ten-week course concentrates on physical and mental fitness and has a 60–80 per cent dropout rate. This overall training process has recently been redesigned to improve training results for CCTs. Having completed the IQTC students move to Key West Florida to undertake the four-week Combat Divers Course followed by three weeks at the Army Airborne School at Fort Benning, Georgia. Students then move to Yuma, Arizona for the Air Force Freefall School, learning HALO/HAHO techniques. Having obtained their parachute wings PJs and combat controllers undertake three-week Combat Survival School at Fairchild Air Force Base, Washington followed by Underwater Escape Training (Dunker) at Naval Air Station Pensacola.

Once these phases have been successfully completed the PJ trainees move to the JFK Special Warfare Center and School at Fort Bragg, North Carolina, to undertake the twenty-four week Army Special Forces Combat Medical and Advance Trauma Medical Courses. At this stage

para-rescuemen undertake a further twenty weeks' training at the Para-rescue School at Kirkland AFB, New Mexico, while combat controllers undertake a three-month Air Traffic Control course for FAA certified ATC qualification before advancing to the thirteen-week Combat Control School at Pope AFB, NC.

At the end of their training para-rescuemen and combat controllers are capable of being inserted into a hostile area in any region of the world from the Arctic to the desert by a variety of methods from HALO/HAHO parachute jump, fast-roping from a helicopter, using boats or SCUBA equipment, vehicle or motorcycle.

Para-rescue personnel can be deployed into a hostile area to search and locate downed aircrew or other casualties and prepare them for extraction by whatever means available. They are also capable of establishing and organising casualty collection, triage and evacuation points. Combat air controllers can be deployed ahead of

The MH-53 Pave Low has been regularly updated over the years and is now the only helicopter operating within the USAF Special Operations Command.

USAF special operations crews and MH-53M Pave Low IV crews conduct their mission training at USAF Special Operations School at Kirkland Air Force Base.

The MH-53M Pave Low IV is well protected with a sophisticated and fully integrated self-defence system including chaff and flares.

ABOVE: A 21st SOS MH-53M Pave Low IV approaching an MC-130P Combat Shadow for in-flight refuelling over flooded Mozambique in 2000.

BELOW: The MH-53M Pave Low IV is due to be replaced by the CV-22.

ABOVE: A pair of 21st SOS MH-53M Pave Low IVs approaching RNoAF Bardufoss in northern Norway during a regular deployment.

BELOW: The MC-130P Combat Shadow specialises in night air-to-air refuelling of Army and Air Force special operations helicopters.

ABOVE: An AC-130 gunship approaches a USAF KC-135 to take on fuel.

BELOW: Designed to provide precision close-in air support the AC-130 gunship is always in high demand from special forces on the ground.

ABOVE: The AC-130 main weapon and targeting systems are located on the port side of the aircraft.

BELOW: This head-on image shows the 105 mm cannon and 40 mm cannon barrels on the port side along with the side-looking low-light and infrared sensor equipment.

or along with special forces to locate, establish and control landing and DZs in the most austere regions of the world as well as establishing forward area refuelling and rearming points (FARRP) for special operations forces helicopters and C-130s. They can also provide terminal attack and control capability in order to designate targets for helicopters or fixed-wing aircraft in a hostile environment. Combat Weather Team (CWT) members, typically assigned to US Army special forces counterparts, provide the ground force commander with critical weather observations and forecasting at the objective area. The combination of all three – PJs, CCTs and CWTs – into the Special Tactics weapons system provides the war-fighting commander with a unique and critical capability when he needs to co-ordinate the air-to-ground interface during special operations missions or provide the special operations enabling force in the conventional battlefield.

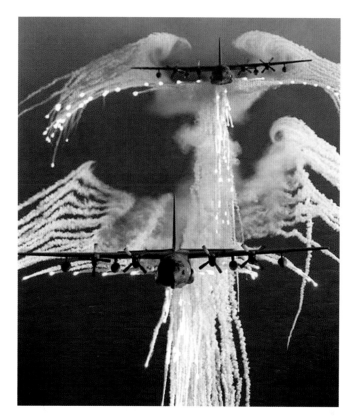

RIGHT: A pair of 67th SOS MC-130P Combat Shadows firing flares.

BELOW: There are two types of AC-130: the Spectre, and the Spooky, the pressurised variant known as the AC-130U or 'U-Boat'.

ABOVE: The MC-130 Combat Talon can deliver equipment to special forces in a number of ways including the LAPs method shown here flown by a C-130.

BELOW: Engineers from the 352nd Maintenance Squadron based at RAF Mildenhall prepare a 7th SOS MC-130H Combat Talon II for a night mission.

MC-130H Combat Talon II pilots can fly their aircraft using a combination of NVGs, TA/TF radar and FLIR displayed on the two colour Multi-Function displays (MFDs).

The Future

Within the next few years the Bell/Boeing CV-22 Osprey, the special operations derivative of the MV-22 Osprey Tilt-Rotor aircraft, will begin to replace the AFSOC MH-53M Pave Low IV along with a number of MC-130H Combat Talon IIs and MC-130P Combat Shadow aircraft. The Air Force has ordered around fifty CV-22 Ospreys. The Osprey will have increased speed, range, and very low-level adverse weather penetration to perform missions normally undertaken using both helicopters and aircraft.

The CV-22 Osprey will transform the way AFSOC conducts its business, enabling true long-range, high speed all-weather covert operations. Other future plans include the development of a stealth gunship, which is smaller, faster and more manoeuvrable than the AC-130, with a better selection of weapons and communications. Other proposals are for an improved EC-130E Commando Solo aircraft based on the Boeing 767 and a stealth equivalent of the MC-130 Combat Talon II. Other options are Unmanned Aerial Vehicles (UAVs) and smaller, lighter and more versatile equipment for special tactics personnel.

FOLLOWING PAGES: Major Thomas Tran from 7th SOS seen flying his MC-130H Combat Talon II on a night training mission in the UK.

ABOVE: A crewman on a 7th SOS MC-130H Combat Talon II waits for
the signal to release a low-level heavy drop of supplies at high speed.

BELOW: A USAF CV-22 Osprey, due to replace the MH-53.

ABOVE: Special Forces Marines seen HALO jumping from a CV-22 Osprey. USAFSOC have ordered fifty aircraft to replace the MH-53.

BELOW: A combat controller jumps from an MC-130 Combat Talon.

ABOVE: USAFSOC combat controllers and para-rescuemen are all free-fall parachute-trained.

BELOW: An MH-53M Pave Low IV being deployed aboard a USAF C-5 Galaxy. Rapid deployment aboard USAF transports is an important requirement for special operations helicopters.

ABOVE: USAFSOC para-rescuemen are all highly trained and can be deployed into any operational theatre with little support, to provide medical aid to special forces and downed aircrew.

RIGHT: Like other special forces operatives, USAFSOC para-rescuemen and combat controllers are equipped for night operations and have secure speech communications.

USAF combat controllers and para-rescuemen undertake a gruelling qualification course requiring physical fitness, stamina and perseverance to even be selected for training.

CHAPTER 7
US Navy SEALs

The US Navy SEALs (Sea, Air, Land specialists) have gained an enviable reputation as one of the most professional and highly trained special operations units within US Special Operations Command. The selection procedure for the SEAL training programme is one of the toughest in the US military, and less than 30 per cent of students graduate. US Navy SEALs are a small and select unit with only around 2200 men operating within SEAL Teams, SEAL Delivery Vehicle (SDV) Teams or Special Boat Squadrons/Special Boat Units. Only around 220 new SEALs per year are needed to fulfil the quota.

SEALs are specialists in all aspects of maritime special forces operations, from deploying covert reconnaissance teams into enemy territory, to undertaking clandestine underwater demolition tasks. As their title explains, SEALs are trained to conduct their missions from either the land, sea or air. Instruction includes attending the US Army

US Navy SEALs have their own dedicated helicopter squadrons HS-4/HS-5 equipped with the Sikorsky HH-60H Strike Hawk.

ABOVE: This Navy HH-60 Sea Hawk is equipped with a nose-mounted FLIR and Hellfire missile, useful for providing SEALs with air support.

BELOW: Navy SEALs fast-roping onto the back of a Mk 5 special operations craft from an HH-60H Strike Hawk.

Basic Airborne School at Fort Benning to gain their parachute wings, before undertaking specialist HALO/HAHO training. Their primary missions are to undertake unconventional warfare anywhere on the globe (including foreign internal defence), direct action, special reconnaissance and counter-terrorist operations.

A Navy SEAL armed with an M4 carbine provides cover during a boat assault training mission.

Naval Special Warfare Command

Located at Coronado Naval Base, San Diego, California, Headquarters, Naval Special Warfare Command is tasked to provide support to naval and joint force special operations and their mission commanders within a theatre of operation. Naval special forces are deployed at various locations around the world, operating within Naval Special Warfare Units, such as Naval Special Warfare Unit 2 located within the European Special Operations Command Group based at Stuttgart, Germany. SEAL units are also organised into two main groups – Western Teams and Eastern Teams. The Western Teams comprise SEAL Team 1, SEAL Team 3 and SEAL Team 5, which are located at Coronado, California. The Eastern Teams comprising SEAL Team 2, SEAL Team 4 and SEAL Team 8 are located

at Little Creek, Norfolk, Virginia. These SEAL Teams were reorganised in 1983 and now include the Naval Special Warfare Development Group, located at Little Creek, Virginia who are responsible for all SEAL 'black' operations including hostage rescue and counter-terrorism. They work alongside US Army Delta and other US Security Agencies. SEALs from this unit deployed with the Rangers and Delta Force to Somalia. The latest unit, SEAL Team 8, are specialists in combat recovery and strike force operations and regularly deploy aboard US aircraft carriers.

SEAL Selection/Training

Selection to the SEALs is open to all active enlisted Navy personnel. Prior to attending the Basic Underwater Demolition (BUD)/SEAL Training School at Coronado,

Navy SEALs heli-casting from a USMC CH-46 Sea Knight with their Zodiac boat.

The Zodiac inflatable boat is popular with special forces and is seen in use by members of SEAL Team 5.

The SEAL training programme is one of the toughest, as demonstrated by this SEAL member, seen about to deploy into the ocean from a submarine during SDV training.

Navy SEALs undertake specialist training including SDV operation as seen here with SEAL Team 2's SDV returning to the mother submarine.

Members of SEAL Team 2 securing their SDV to the mother submarine during training in the Caribbean Sea.

California, all prospective candidates attend a five-day familiarisation course at the Naval Training Command, Great Lakes followed by two weeks of pre-conditioning and indoctrination before being allowed to progress. This process eliminates those who have not fully prepared for the physical and mental challenges ahead.

BUD/SEAL Training lasts for twenty-five weeks and is undertaken in three phases. It is one of the most demanding training courses in the world.

Phase 1
Phase 1 comprises eight weeks of continual hard physical activity including timed runs in boots on the beach,

two-mile swims, obstacle courses, multiple individual challenges and tasks. This culminates in 'Hell' week (week five) when students are put through five days of continuous training with fewer than four hours' sleep, taken in one-hour blocks. Passing this phase proves a student's commitment to joining the SEALs. The remaining three weeks are taken up with teaching hydrographic reconnaissance and surveys.

Phase 2
This phase concentrates on combat SCUBA diving using open- (air) and closed- (oxygen) circuit diving techniques to undertake long-distance underwater dives and learning various covert techniques. The physical training regime continues.

Phase 3
This ten-week phase takes place on San Clement Island

An SDV returning to the mother submarine. The SDV is an important asset in covert deployment and recovery of SEAL Teams.

and concentrates on land warfare techniques, navigation, field craft skills, helicopter operations (including roping, rappelling and heli-casting), underwater explosives, river and stream operations and covert reconnaissance techniques. This can also include attending Ranger School at Fort Benning.

Having graduated from BUD/SEAL training, graduates attend Basic Army Parachute School at Fort Benning prior to joining their SEAL Team to complete a six-month probation. SEALs then undertake specialist training to become qualified, for example, as Diving Supervisors, language experts, Snipers, SEAL Delivery Vehicle (SDV) operators, weapons or communications experts or HAHO/HALO qualified.

SEAL Team

SEAL Teams normally comprise ten 16-man platoons that can operate autonomously and conduct reconnaissance, direct action, unconventional warfare. They can operate in any environment including maritime or riverine.

SEAL Delivery Vehicle Team

These teams operate and maintain SEAL Delivery Vehicles and other submersible systems that deliver and recover SEALs in hostile areas. SEAL Teams and SDV elements are capable of limited shallow-water, mine clearing operations and are transported by a mother submarine.

Special Boat Units

These units operate a number of coastal and river patrol boats including 40 ft RIBs and Mark Five Special Operations Craft. They undertake a full range of missions including counter-drug operations.

A SEAL Team aboard an inflatable boat on a raiding mission carrying their fins strapped to their backs.

BUD/SEAL training is conducted at the Naval Special Warfare Center at Coronado and includes 'surf passage' training as shown here.

SEALs operate a number of specialist boats including the Mark Five Assault Craft seen here equipped with a 0.50 in cannon.

OPPOSITE: Members of SEAL Team 2 seen aboard a USN submarine in the Caribbean Sea. SEALs use subs and helicopters to carry out their clandestine missions.

ABOVE: Navy SEALs operating a rigid-hull inflatable boat seen during a hostage-rescue training mission in New York.

LEFT: A heavily armed Navy SEAL Special Boat Unit seen patrolling a river system, one of their many roles.

CHAPTER 8
US Marine Corps Special Operations Capable Units

Although not formally part of US Special Operations Command, the US Marine Corps comes under the umbrella of Naval Special Warfare Command and retains special operations-capable trained units, known as Maritime Special Purpose Forces, as part of their standard Marine Expeditionary Unit (MEU). Both aviation and marine infantry units undertake special operations training, specialising in a variety of night missions including amphibious deep-strike raids, Military Operations in Urban Terrain (MOUT), Tactical Recovery of Aircraft and Personnel/Combat Search and Rescue (TRAP/CSAR) and counter-terrorist missions including hostage rescue. This training takes place at Camp Lejeune, North Carolina, and Camp Pendleton, California, with US Marine Corps units and personnel participating in various specialised training programmes conducted by units within USSOC. Marines regularly undertake the Ranger training course as well as US Army Airborne School.

US Marines conduct their own specialised reconnaissance training with the Amphibious Reconnaissance School at Fort Story, Virginia. This nine-week course takes students to Fort Story, Fort A.P. Hill and Key West, Florida. Students undertake training in small boat handling, hydrographic and beach reconnaissance, nautical and land navigation, helicopter operations including roping and rappelling, photography, sketching, patrolling, communications and basic demolitions. The school also runs the Reconnaissance Scout Swimmer Course (undertaken by LRRPU and Army Special Forces) and Reconnaissance Operations Planning Courses.

US Marines special forces fast-rope from a CH-46E Sea Knight during a hostage-rescue training mission.

A USMC CH-53E from HMH-464 about to deploy a USMC special operations team onto the embassy roof in Combat Town, Camp Lejeune, North Carolina.

FOLLOWING PAGES: Like the ground Marines, USMC aviators undertake special operations capable training to be able to support special operations missions.

Like other US special operations helicopters, this CH-53E is equipped with a nose-mounted FLIR system for night missions.

Soon to become a permanent unit with USSOC, the USMC has valuable experience in maritime and amphibious special operations including air-to-air refuelling.

OPPOSITE AND ABOVE: A pair of CH-53Es from HMH-464 refuels from a USMC KC-130 tanker during a long-range low-level TRAP/CSAR training mission.

ABOVE: US Marines from the Amphibious Force Reconnaissance Unit swim ashore with their equipment to take up their observation positions.

LEFT: A member of the Amphibious Force Reconnaissance Unit fast-roping from a CH-46E Sea Knight during a Maritime Counter-Terrorist (MCT) training mission.

OPPOSITE: A patrol deploys from a CH-53E during special operations capable training in Southern California. In October 2001 the 15th MEU (SOC) was doing this for real in Afghanistan.

ABOVE: A Marine from 'Force Recon' aiming his M-230-equipped M-16A1.

LEFT: A Marine sniper from 'Force Recon' taking aim from his hide.

US Marine special operations capable units are deployed aboard a variety of amphibious ships, forming a Marine Expeditionary Unit (SOC) and are deployed ready to undertake a full range of special operations missions anywhere in the world.

CHAPTER 9
Operation *Enduring Freedom* – Afghanistan

The speed and success of Operation *Enduring Freedom*, launched in response to the terrorist attacks on New York and Washington in September 2001, and the leading role played by the United States Special Operations Command will change the way the United States conducts future military operations. The success of the joint operation in Afghanistan involving units from the Army, Air Force, Navy and United States Marine Corps, and the devastating combination of Special Operations forces and airpower has already changed US military doctrine.

The mission helped to reaffirm the stringent training and operational doctrine of Special Operations, using all the specialised skills and experiences accumulated by special forces units over the past twenty years. The professionalism and versatility of special forces units on the ground dramatically increased the effectiveness of the air campaign, operating in their special reconnaissance and direct-action roles to designate and mark targets for precision laser-guided and JDAM bombs. In their foreign internal defence/unconventional warfare roles they helped to turn the Northern Alliance into a conquering army. Special forces liaison teams provided equipment, training and tactical support to the Northern Alliance and Afghan militia. The teams' preparation for this included foreign language courses and training for operations in that particular geographical area.

Special forces teams from the 5th Special Forces Group (Airborne) along with SEAL teams and US Air Force Special Tactics personnel were supported by United States Special Operations Aviation Units operating AC-130s, MC-130H Combat Talons and MH-53M Pave Lows as they assisted the Northern Alliance and Afghan militia in their campaign to remove the Taliban forces and locate Osama Bin Laden and the Al-Qaeda forces.

On 20 October 2001 the 75th Ranger Regiment (Airborne) undertook a night parachute raid south of Kandahar to assault two objectives, followed by a Combat Recovery of a downed helicopter crew and the recovery of civilian hostages held by the Taliban. The United States Marine Corps, 15th Marine Expeditionary Unit (Special Operations Capable) deployed to an area south-west of Kandahar and established Camp Rhino before securing Kandahar airport, whilst also undertaking 'Hunter-Killer' missions to track down Al-Qaeda units. Special forces teams working alongside Afghan troops then conducted missions to seek out Osama Bin Laden and Al-Qaeda troops, who were believed to be hiding in the Tora Bora mountain range.

A USMC CH-46E Sea Knight landing at Camp Rhino.

ABOVE; A US Defense Department-released image of US special forces soldiers riding on horseback alongside Afghan Northern Alliance troops.

With the future emphasis on 'The War Against Terrorism' and the United States doctrine of more-easily deployable, smaller, harder-hitting forces relying on modern technology and better training, the role of United States Special Operations Command will expand. The command represents only 1.3 per cent of the United States Department of Defense with a total number of 40,000 SEALs, Army Special Forces and Air Force Commandos and uses only 1.3 per cent of the defence budget, providing US taxpayers with good value for their money and a dedicated and professional special operations force.

RIGHT: A USMC CH-53E pilot checks his helicopter at Camp Rhino prior to a mission.

USMC 15th and 26th MEU (SOC) marines at an encampment outside
Kandahar.

US Army special forces equipment carried by Northern Alliance mules.

Suspected Taliban prisoners being searched by US marines at Kandahar.

ABOVE: USMC 15th MEU (SOC) marines establishing a forward base at Camp Rhino in Afghanistan.

BELOW: USMC AH-1W Cobras refuelling at Camp Rhino whilst being prepared for operations by US Navy engineers.

INDEX